Multiplication & Division Activity Book

for ages 8-9

This CGP book is bursting with fun activities to build up children's skills and confidence.

It's ideal for extra practice to reinforce their learning in primary school. Enjoy!

Published by CGP

Editors:
Michael Bushell, Ruth Greenhalgh, Tom Miles and Rosa Roberts

Proofreaders:
Joanne Haslett and David Ryan

With thanks to Lottie Edwards for the copyright research.

ISBN: 978 1 78908 624 9

Graphics used on the cover and throughout the book © www.edu~clips.com
Cover design concept by emc design ltd.

Printed by Elanders Ltd, Newcastle upon Tyne.

Contents

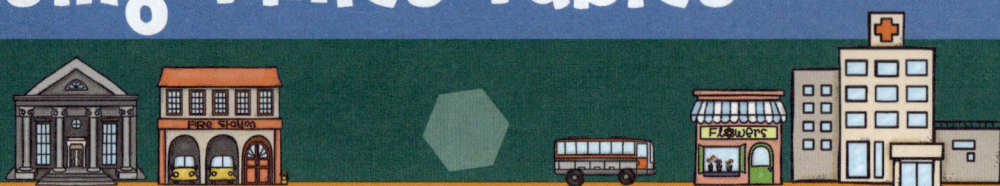

Using Times Tables

How It Works

You'll need to know your times tables to answer the problems on these pages. Look inside the back cover if you need a reminder. Here's an example:

A hospital treated **6** sore ribs and **7** scuffed knees each day, for **3** days. How many of each did the hospital treat in total?

3 × 6 = 18 sore ribs   **3 × 7 = 21** scuffed knees

Now Try These

1. Draw lines to match each person with the cause of their injury.

5 × 9   4 × 11   5 × 7   6 × 6

44   36   45   35

2. Circle the calculation which gives the biggest answer.

9 × 3   2 × 12   5 × 6   3 × 11   4 × 7

3. Every year, Ebele rescues 7 cats from trees and 8 rabbits from wells.

a) How many cats does she rescue in 6 years?

b) How many rabbits does she rescue in 7 years?

.... cats

.... rabbits

4. Fill in the missing numbers.

$3 \times 12 = $ ☐

☐ $\times 9 = 18$

☐ $\times 12 = 60$

$6 \times$ ☐ $= 66$

5. Derek is buying these items for his barber shop.

comb

scissors

broom

Work out the cost of buying:

a) 4 brooms,

b) 8 combs,

c) 9 scissors.

£ ....

£ ....

£ ....

An Extra Challenge

Sarah needs to deliver these parcels. Each multiplication tells you the house number.

11 × 11

8 × 9

12 × 12

7 × 9

12 × 7

11 × 12

Draw a path by connecting dots on the roads below to deliver all the parcels.

- You must go through each dot exactly once.
- You must pass in front of a house number to deliver to that address.

How was that? Did you do a good job with multiplying?

😕 ☐   🙂 ☐   😉 ☐

3

More Times Tables

How It Works

Times tables can be used to answer division problems — here's an example:

Dawn needs **6** logs to make a fire. How many fires can she make with **42** logs?

$7 \times 6 = 42$ means that $42 \div 6 = 7$. So Dawn can make **7** fires.

If the numbers don't divide exactly, you'll have some objects left over. For example:

Sarah also needs **6** logs to make a fire. She has **50** logs.
How many fires can she make? How many logs will she have left over?

50 isn't in the 6 times table, so find the highest number of 6s that are less than 50. ⟶ $8 \times 6 = 48$, so Sarah can make **8 fires**.

Subtract to find the number of logs left. ⟶ $50 - 48 = 2$, so Sarah has **2 logs** left over.

Now Try These

1. Fill in the missing numbers.

$48 \div 6 = \boxed{}$

$\boxed{} \div 6 = 4$

$56 \div 7 = \boxed{}$

$\boxed{} \div 7 = 9$

2. Phoebe needs to catch 4 fish to make a fish pie.

a) On Monday, she catches 36 fish. How many pies can she make?

.... pies

b) On Tuesday, she catches 27 fish.
How many pies can she make? How many fish does she have left over?

.... pies   .... fish left over

3. When the villagers below divide the number they are thinking of by their pet's number, they get their hut's number. Match each villager with their pet and hut.

99

35

9

7

5

84

7

12

11

4. Greg can make 1 ice sculpture in 9 hours.
How many complete sculptures could he make in 30 hours?

.... sculptures

5. 20 villagers are going for a trip down a river in boats.
Each boat can hold up to 7 people. How many boats are needed?

Think carefully —
you can't leave
anyone behind!

.... boats

An Extra Challenge

Greg is frozen in ice! Solve the clues to guide Inga to him. Where is he?

- First take the path that can be divided by 6.

- Then follow the number missing from $49 ÷ ? = 7$.

- To find the final number, answer this problem:

How many choc-ices does each person get if 121 choc-ices are shared equally between 11 people?

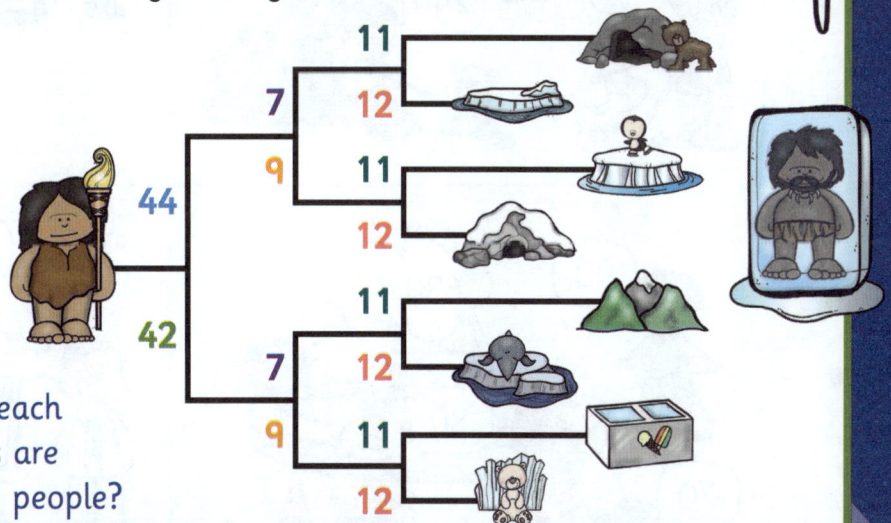

44

42

7

9

11

12

11

12

11

7

12

9

11

12

11

12

How were these pages?
Did you keep your cool?

Times Tables Tricks

How It Works

Knowing your times tables helps you do all sorts of harder calculations. For example, here's how you could find **600 ÷ 3**:

You know **6 ÷ 3 = 2**. 600 is 100 times bigger than **6**, so the answer to **600 ÷ 3** will be **100 times bigger** than the answer to **6 ÷ 3**.

6 ÷ 3 = 2
600 ÷ 3 = 200
So the answer is **200**.

Now Try These

1. Do this training exercise to earn your secret agent badge.

    a) 40 × 7   b) 90 ÷ 3

    ....

2. In each scene, a spy is listening for someone to say a secret number. Colour the speech bubble that matches the number each spy is thinking about.

3. Work out:

a) 500 × 4

....

b) 11 × 800

....

c) 630 ÷ 9

....

d) 600 ÷ 12

....

4. Agent Scorpion goes to a gadget shop.

 **£12**

binoculars

 **£7**

disguise

 **£300**

watch

a) He buys 60 binoculars and 9 watches.
How much did he spend on each?

Binoculars:

£ ....

Watches:

£ ....

b) He also spent £490 on disguises.
How many did he buy?

.... disguises

An Extra Challenge

Agent Mongoose knows one of these jewels is fake.
Use the clues to help her figure out which one it is.

- The price of the fake jewel <u>cannot</u> be divided by 500.

- The price of the fake jewel <u>can</u> be divided by 900.

- The price of the fake jewel <u>cannot</u> be divided by 400.

 **£3600**

 **£4200**

 **£4500**

 **£5400**

How did it go? Did you uncover
any times tables secrets?

😕 ☐   🙂 ☐   😉 ☐

More Times Tables Tricks

You can **multiply three numbers** by picking any two to multiply first, then multiplying the result by the third number. Here's an example:

Hades has **4** dogs. Each dog has **3** heads and each head has **2** ears. How many ears do the dogs have in total?

This is asking for **4** × **3** × **2**. You could calculate this as:

$$4 \times 3 \times 2 = 4 \times 6 = 24 \quad \text{or} \quad 4 \times 3 \times 2 = 12 \times 2 = 24$$

You could even swap the order, e.g. $4 \times 3 \times 2 = 2 \times 3 \times 4$.

Whichever way you do it, you'll get the same answer: **24 ears**.

Now Try These

1. Multiply the numbers along each line. One has been done for you.

40

$4 \times 5 \times 2 = 40$

2

5

5

7

4

4

1

4

0

5

2

6

9

2

4

7

2. Work out:

$584 \times 1 = $ .... $719 \times 0 = $ .... $263 \div 1 = $ ....

3. Work out these calculations.

a) 2 × 9 × 6

b) 3 × 7 × 4

c) 5 × 8 × 7

4. Medusa is turning people to stone! But they can be protected by a magical shield.
   Write the answer to each multiplication on the shields to make them magical.

 5 × 11 × 4

6 × 12 × 5

5. Hercules jogs 3 miles, 4 times every day. How far does he jog in:

a) 12 days?

b) 40 days?

.... miles

.... miles

An Extra Challenge

The Minotaur is hungry and he's a fussy eater.
He wants 3 pieces of fruit that multiply
together to make 360.

Find a path to the Minotaur that passes over the
correct fruit. How many ways can you feed him?

No backtracking is allowed.

Factor Pairs

How It Works

A **factor** of a number is another whole number that divides it exactly.
Two factors that multiply together to give the number are called a **factor pair**.

For example: **12 ÷ 3 = 4** and **12 ÷ 4 = 3**,
so **3** and **4** are both factors of **12**.
They're a factor pair as **3 × 4 = 12**.

> If you know one factor, you can just divide by it to find the other factor in the pair.

A factor pair can tell you two different ways to **share** things **equally**.

6 plasters can be shared into **2** lots of **3**...   ... or into **3** lots of **2**.

   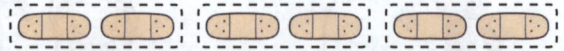

Now Try These

1. Fill in the boxes to complete the factor pairs.

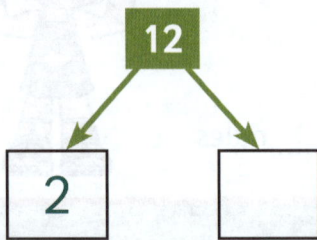   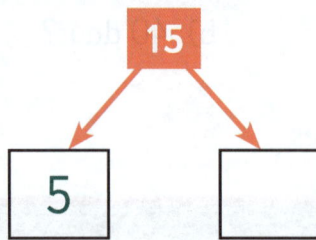   

12	
2	

15	
5	

21	
7	

2. Draw lines to match each person with a balloon and a landing place to make a factor pair of their number. One has been done for you.

3   5   6   2

5   6   5   11

3. Fill in the missing number on each boat so that the first two numbers are a factor pair of the third number.

5   [   ]   60

7   8   [   ]

4. a) Fill in the missing numbers to write all factor pairs of 18.

   1 and 18   .... and .... and ....

   b) Salma has 18 skiing trophies. She wants to split them into equal groups, with more than one in each group. How many different ways can she do this?   ....

5. Logan teaches 20 people how to walk a tightrope. He splits them into equal classes, with each class having at least two people.

   How many people are in each class? Circle all the possible answers.

   1   2   3   4   5   6   7   8   9   10

An Extra Challenge

Jamie is diving in a shark cage, but the shark is getting a little bit too friendly!

To distract the shark, select worms from below to put on the hooks so that each number points to a factor pair below it.

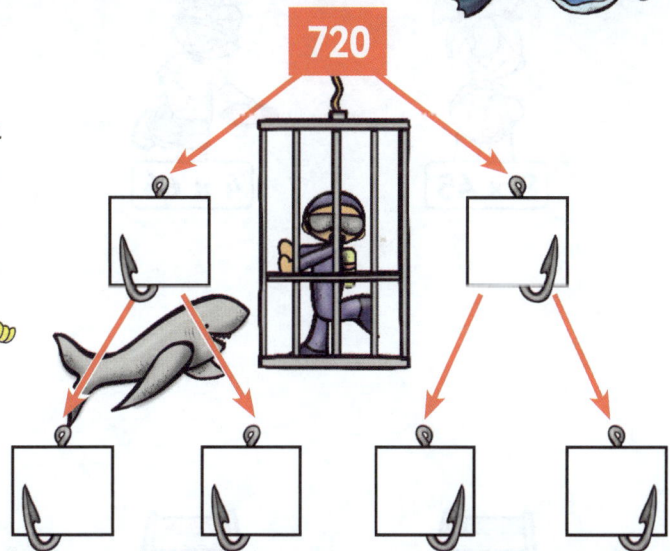

50   3   60   12

20   9   6   2

720

Tick a box. Go outside the lines if you're feeling extreme!

11

Multiplying Using Partitioning

How It Works

You can use **partitioning** to turn a tricky multiplication problem into one that can be worked out using **times tables**. Here's how:

What is **7 × 34**?

$34 = \textbf{30} + \textbf{4}$ ←— Split 34 into tens and ones.

$7 × \textbf{30} = 210$ and $7 × \textbf{4} = 28$ ←— Multiply each part separately.

$210 + 28 = \textbf{238}$ ←— Add the results together.

Now Try These

1. Use partitioning to work out:

a) $32 × 6 = \boxed{} × 6 + \boxed{} × 6$

$= \boxed{} + \boxed{}$

$= \boxed{}$

b) $56 × 7$

2. Draw lines to match each person with their beach chair.

8 × 45   4 × 64   5 × 92   6 × 49

256   460   360   294

3. A day trip to a beach resort costs £27 for children and £32 for adults.
   What is the total cost for:

   a) 9 children?　　　　　　　　　　b) 8 adults?

   £ .... 　　　　　　　　　　£ ....

4. Write the missing numbers in the boxes.

   $215 \times 3 =$ [200] $\times 3 +$ [10] $\times 3 +$ [ ] $\times 3$

   $=$ [600] $+$ [ ] $+$ [ ] $=$ [ ]

   $172 \times 4 =$ [ ] $\times 4 +$ [ ] $\times 4 +$ [ ] $\times 4$

   $=$ [ ] $+$ [ ] $+$ [ ] $=$ [ ]

5. A cafe sells 125 portions of fish 'n' chips each week.
   How many portions does it sell in 5 weeks?

   .... portions

An Extra Challenge

Larry's ice cream van sells the types of ice cream shown below.
One day he sells 25 each of three different types. He earns £300.
Circle three types of ice cream that he could have sold that day.

£3　　£9　　£2　　£8

£4　　£7　　£5

How did it go? Are you
partitioning like a pro?

13

Kooky Card Game

Raj and Abi are **taking it in turns** to play against Hanna in a card game. Hanna has some **character cards** and some **maths** cards.

In each round, Hanna must put down **one card of each type**, and Raj or Abi do the same. The player with the **higher score** wins the round.

To work out a score, you **apply** the instruction on the **maths card** to the number on the **character card**. For example:

- If Hanna plays Spaghettling with '**×3**', she scores: **32 × 3 = 96**.

- If Hanna plays Dr Cyclops with '**÷8**', she scores: **72 ÷ 8 = 9**.

Here are the cards Raj and Abi play in Round 1 and Round 2:

Round 1 — Raj   Round 2 — Abi

Hanna has the 5 cards below to use in Rounds 1 and 2. She must play <u>one character</u> and <u>one maths</u> card in each round. Cards can only be used once.

She <u>wins both rounds</u>. Which cards does she play in each round?

Make a note of the round you think Hanna plays the cards in. You can record the results in the score sheet on the next page.

Hanna has some different cards for Round 3 and Round 4:

Dr Cyclops	Butter Bye Bye	The Pattersons	Maths $\div 2$	Maths $\div 6$
72	90	48	☐	☐
☐	☐	☐		

Here are the cards Raj and Abi play in Rounds 3 and 4:

Round 3 — Raj

Maths $\div 4$

The Universe

160

Round 4 — Abi

Maths $\div 7$

Tim the Turkey

63

Hanna <u>wins Round 3</u> but <u>loses Round 4</u>.
Which cards does she play in Round 3 and Round 4?

SCORE SHEET

Round 1: Raj's score: .... Hanna's score: ....

Round 2: Abi's score: .... Hanna's score: ....

Round 3: Raj's score: .... Hanna's score: ....

Round 4: Abi's score: .... Hanna's score: ....

The Grid Method

How It Works

The **grid method** can be used to multiply bigger numbers:

What is **175 × 3**?

1) Draw a **grid**. Put the number that you're multiplying by at the **top**.

2) **Partition 175** and write the numbers down the left side.

×	3
100	300
70	210
5	15
	525

3) Fill in the grid. **Multiply** each number on the **left** by the number at the **top**.

4) **Add** the answers up.

Now Try These

1. Write in the missing numbers to complete these multiplications.

180 × 6

×	6
100	600
80	

192 × 5

×	5
100	
90	450
2	

263 × 4

×	4
200	
60	240
3	

2. Some butterflies have been caught. Fill in the grids, then draw lines to match each multiplication to the correct answer to break the cage and set them free.

1064

×	3
300	
40	
7	

×	7
100	
50	
2	

×	8
100	
20	
6	

1008

1041

3. When the cocoon on the left is ready, it will turn into a butterfly. Do the calculation on the cocoon and tick the box next to the butterfly it will become.

483 × 6

×	

☐ 2838

☐ 2898

☐ 2904

4. Renee and Tim bought some T-shirts from a gift shop.

£9   £8   £6

a) Renee bought 39 Earth T-shirts. How much did she spend?

b) Tim bought 124 butterfly T-shirts. How much did he spend?

£ ....

£ ....

An Extra Challenge

Azizi and Marie see the butterflies shown below in a butterfly garden.

They're told that the garden has 27 times more butterflies than the number they see.

How many butterflies does the garden have in total?

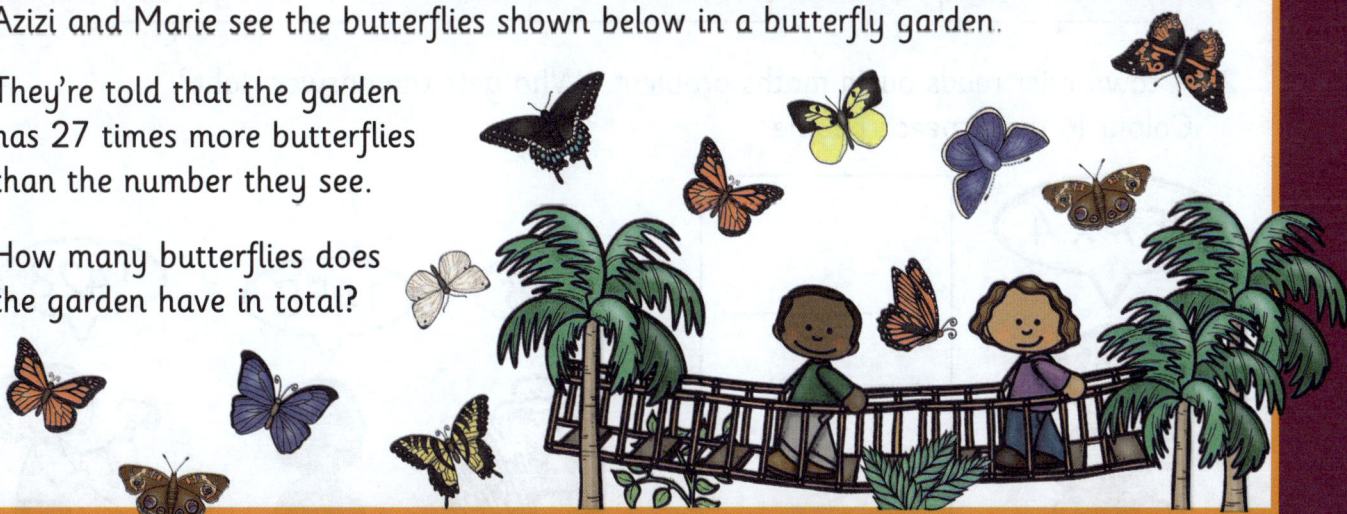

Written Multiplication 1

You can also multiply using **columns**. Here's how:

What is **246 × 4**?

Write the numbers in columns of hundreds, tens and ones. Put the **bigger** number on top.

Multiply the **ones** in 246 by 4. ⟶ $6 \times 4 =$

Multiply the **tens** by 4. ⟶ $40 \times 4 =$

Then multiply the ⟶ $200 \times 4 =$ **hundreds** by the 4.

	H	T	O
	2	**4**	**6**
×			**4**
		2	**4**
	1	**6**	**0**
	8	**0**	**0**
	9	**8**	**4**

Finally, **add up** the numbers in each column.

$4 + 0 + 0 = 4$

$2 + 6 + 0 = 8$

$1 + 8 = 9$ ⟵

Now Try These

1. Work out these calculations:

```
    6 5
×     7
_____

_____
```

```
    8 9
×     2
_____

_____
```

```
    3 6
×     9
_____

_____
```

2. A town crier reads out a maths problem. Who gets the answer right? Colour in their speech bubble.

357 × 4

```
×
_____

_____
```

1398   1458   1428

3. Match each pair of shoes with an item used to help make them.
   Write the correct letter in each box on the right.

A	189 × 6
B	267 × 4
C	352 × 3

☐ 1056

☐ 1134

☐ 1068

4. Solve these problems.

```
      7 4 2
  ×       3
  _____
```

```
      4 9 4
  ×       5
  _____
```

```
      5 1 7
  ×       8
  _____
```

An Extra Challenge

A farmer has four different types of chicken.
The boxes show the number she has of each.

The nests show the eggs that **one** chicken of
each type has laid. Each chicken of the same
type has laid the **same** number of eggs.

Which type has laid
the **largest** number of
eggs in total?

93 Super Cluckers

268 Snowies

194 Fancy Feathers

157 Red Hens

'Ey now, 'ow was that? Some
smashin' pages or not fer you?

😕 ☐   🙂 ☐   😉 ☐

Written Multiplication 2

How It Works

Short multiplication is like the method on the previous page, but you don't write the steps on different rows. Here's how to do it:

What is **246 × 4**?

1) Write the numbers with the hundreds, tens and ones in columns. Put the **bigger** number on top.

```
  H T O
    2 4 6
  ×     4
  _____
    9 8 4
    1 2
```

2) First, multiply the **ones** by 4.

> 6 × 4 = **24**. Write the **4 ones** in the ones column and the **2 tens** below the line in the tens column.

3) Then multiply the **tens** by 4.

> 40 × 4 = **160**, so add **6 tens** to the **2 tens** from the last step to give **8** in the tens column. Then put the **1 hundred** below the line in the hundreds column.

4) Finally, multiply the **hundreds** by 4.

> 200 × 4 = **800**, so add **8 hundreds** to the **1 hundred** that's already in the hundreds column to get **9 hundreds**.

Now Try These

1. Use each number in the box **once** to fill in the gaps in the multiplications.

```
      8 3
  ×     6
  _____
  4 ..... 8
    .....
```

```
    1 9 7
  ×     4
  _____
  7 ..... 8
    ..... .....
```

```
    4 5 8
  ×     3
  _____
  ..... 3 ..... .....
      ..... 2
```

Box of numbers:
8 1 9 1 3
7 4 1 2

2. Una and David want to take the shortest route to a dig site. The lengths of different routes are given by these calculations. Tick the route they should take.

☐ Dino Dunes

```
    1 5 7
  ×     8
  _____
```

☐ Paleo Path

```
    1 3 2
  ×     9
  _____
```

☐ T-Rex Road

```
    2 4 4
  ×     6
  _____
```

3. There's a fake fossil at a museum.
   Its museum number is equal to 376 × 3. Circle the fake fossil.

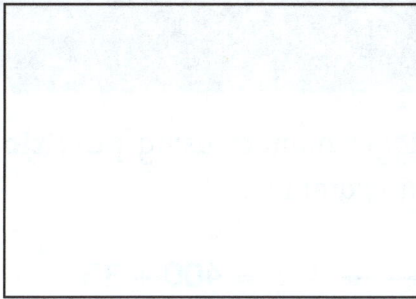

1108

1128

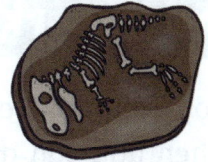
1228

4. A team found 162 dinosaur bones at Site A. At Site B, they found 9 times as many bones.

   How many bones did they find at Site B?

5. Alex bought 7 spades. Each spade cost £348.

   How much did she spend in total?

.... bones

£ ....

An Extra Challenge

A fossil of a newly discovered species has been found in the sand.

The fossil is in the square on the grid whose number above and number to the left multiply to give 324.

Which is the fossil from the new species?

	4	5	6	7	8	9
35						
36						
37						
38						

Was this something you could dig your teeth into? Tick a box.

Dividing Using Partitioning

How It Works

You can make a division **easier** by splitting up the bigger number using **partitioning**. Then you can divide **each part** separately. Here's an example:

Work out **435 ÷ 5**.

Split 435 into numbers that can easily be divided by 5. → **435 = 400 + 35**

Divide each part by 5. → **400 ÷ 5 = 80**
35 ÷ 5 = 7

Add together the parts. → So **435 ÷ 5 = 80 + 7 = 87**

Now Try These

1. Fill in these boxes and complete the calculations.

318 ÷ 3

318 = 300 + 18

300 ÷ 3 = ☐

18 ÷ 3 = ☐

So 318 ÷ 3 = ...

824 ÷ 4

824 = 800 + 24

800 ÷ 4 = ☐

24 ÷ 4 = ☐

So 824 ÷ 4 = ...

2. Use partitioning to work out:

a) 96 ÷ 6

b) 85 ÷ 5

c) 91 ÷ 7

....

....

....

3. Draw lines to match up each division with the correct answer.

$118 \div 2$ $428 \div 4$ $336 \div 3$ $255 \div 5$

107   51   112   59

4. A team of pigeons has an important letter to deliver.
   They have to travel 315 km in total. They share the distance equally.

a) How far would each pigeon need
   to fly with 3 pigeons in the team?

b) How far would each pigeon need
   to fly with 5 pigeons in the team?

.... km

.... km

An Extra Challenge

Vinnie the vulture wants to work out a division.

What is $371 \div 7$?

This gaggle of geese suggests calculations he could use to partition his division.
Circle the two that are useful, and work out the answer to Vinnie's problem.

 $350 \div 7$  $300 \div 7$  $320 \div 7$

  $51 \div 7$  $21 \div 7$  $71 \div 7$

How did these pages go? Are
you flying ahead of the pack?

Written Division

How It Works

You can also divide using short division.
For example, you'd set up **532 ÷ 4** like this:

$$4\overline{)5\ 3\ 2}$$

You'll write your answer on top of the line.

Divide each digit in **532** by 4 separately, starting on the left.

1) **5 hundreds ÷ 4 = 1 hundred** with **1 hundred** left over.

$$4\overline{)5\ {}^13\ 2}$$
$$1$$

2) **13 tens ÷ 4 = 3 tens** with **1 ten** left over.

$$4\overline{)5\ {}^13\ {}^12}$$
$$1\ 3$$

3) **12 ones ÷ 4 = 3 ones**.

$$4\overline{)5\ {}^13\ {}^12}$$
$$1\ 3\ 3$$

The answer is the number on the top of the line when you've finished: 532 ÷ 4 = **133**.

Now Try These

1. Fill in the boxes to work out these divisions.

72 ÷ 4 → ☐ ☐ / 4 ☐ 7 ☐ 2

98 ÷ 7 → ☐ ☐ / ☐ ☐ ☐ ☐

84 ÷ 6 → ☐ ☐ / ☐ ☐ ☐ ☐

2. Use short division to find the answers to these calculations.

$$5\overline{)5\ 5\ 5}$$

$$7\overline{)9\ 4\ 5}$$

$$4\overline{)6\ 8\ 4}$$

$$6\overline{)8\ 0\ 4}$$

3. **Three** of these divisions have the same answer. Circle all three of them.

$560 \div 5$

Use these boxes to do your working out.

$448 \div 4$

$784 \div 7$

$226 \div 2$

4. There are 376 places to pitch a tent in a camp site. These are divided equally between 4 fields.

Use short division to work out how many places are in each field.

.... places

An Extra Challenge

126 campers are going on a wildlife tour. The leaflet below explains how they need to split into groups.

WILLDLIFE TOUR RULES

FOLLOW ME

- There must be more than one camper in each group

- Each group must have an equal number of campers.

a) Could they get into groups of 2? How many groups would there be if they did?

b) What about groups of 3? Is that possible?

c) What other sizes of group could there be? Find as many as you can.

Did written division go well or do you feel lost in the woods?

Real-Life Problems

How It Works

For problems set in the **real world**, you'll need to work out which calculations to do for yourself. Take a look at this example.

Kalil has **96** letters to deliver to **3** streets. Each street receives an equal number of letters. It takes **8** seconds to deliver each letter.

How long does it take to deliver one street's letters?

First, **divide by 3** to find out how many letters each street gets.

$96 = 90 + 6$

$90 ÷ 3 = 30$ and $6 ÷ 3 = 2$
So $96 ÷ 3 = 30 + 2 = 32$

Then **multiply by 8** to find how long one street takes.

$32 = 30 + 2$

$30 × 8 = 240$ and $2 × 8 = 16$
So $32 × 8 = 240 + 16 = 256$

So it takes **256 seconds**.

Now Try These

1. Patty and her 7 friends are posting invitations to a big party.

   a) They're each given 145 invitations to post.
      How many invitations is this altogether?

      .... invitations

   b) They receive 531 envelopes containing replies.
      Three people open them. They open an equal number of replies each.

      How many replies do they each open?

      .... replies

2. Each person who comes to Patty's party donates £8 to a charity.
   490 people come to the party.

   How much money does the charity raise?

   £ ....

3. There are 62 tables at the party. Each table has 8 chairs around it to begin with.

   When all 490 people at the party are sitting down, the spare chairs are taken away. Circle the group with the correct number of spare chairs below.

   Do your working here.

4. The party lasts 5 hours.
   If each song that the DJ plays lasts 3 minutes, how many songs are played at the party?

   There are 60 minutes in 1 hour.

   .... songs

An Extra Challenge

Jamie is buying balloons for a party.
They come in three different sized bunches, as shown below.

Small

Large

Medium

Jamie orders 346 balloons altogether. He orders 24 small bunches and 13 large bunches. How many medium bunches does he order?

Tick a box. Then it's time to celebrate the end of the book!

Answers

Pages 2-3 — Using Times Tables

1. 5×9 —— 45 4×11 —— 44
   5×7 —— 35 6×6 —— 36

2. $9 \times 3 = 27$ $2 \times 12 = 24$ $5 \times 6 = 30$
   $3 \times 11 = 33$ $4 \times 7 = 28$ So **3 × 11** is the biggest.

3. a) $7 \times 6 = 42$ cats   b) $8 \times 7 = 56$ rabbits

4. $3 \times 12 = 36$ $2 \times 9 = 18$ $5 \times 12 = 60$ $6 \times 11 = 66$

5. a) £$9 \times 4 =$ £36   b) £$6 \times 8 =$ £48   c) £$7 \times 9 =$ £63

An Extra Challenge

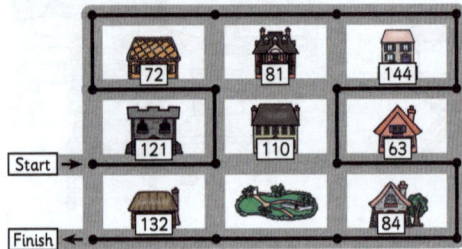

Pages 4-5 — More Times Tables

1. $48 \div 6 = 8$ $56 \div 7 = 8$ $24 \div 6 = 4$ $63 \div 7 = 9$

2. a) $36 \div 4 = 9$ pies
   b) $6 \times 4 = 24$, $27 - 4 = 3$
      So she can make **6 pies** with **3 fish left over**.

3. 99 —— 11 —— 9   84 —— 12 —— 7
   35 —— 7 —— 5

4. $3 \times 9 = 27$, $30 - 27 = 3$, so he can make
   3 complete sculptures (with 3 hours left over).

5. $2 \times 7 = 14$, so 2 boats aren't enough. $3 \times 7 = 21$,
   so **3** boats are enough — 2 full boats of 7 people,
   and 1 boat holding 6 people.

An Extra Challenge

$42 \div 6 = 7$, so take path 42. Then $49 \div 7 = 7$, so
take path 7. Finally, $121 \div 11 = 11$, so take path 11.
Greg is frozen in the mountains (🏔).

Pages 6-7 — Times Tables Tricks

1. a) $4 \times 7 = 28$, so $40 \times 7 = 280$
   b) $9 \div 3 = 3$, so $90 \div 3 = 30$

2. Top left: $12 \times 3 = 36$, so $12 \times 30 = 360$
   Top right: $30 \div 6 = 5$, so $300 \div 6 = 50$
   Bottom left: $63 \div 7 = 9$, so $630 \div 7 = 90$
   Bottom right: $4 \times 11 = 44$, so $40 \times 11 = 440$

3. a) $5 \times 4 = 20$, so $500 \times 4 = 2000$
   b) $11 \times 8 = 88$, so $11 \times 800 = 8800$
   c) $63 \div 9 = 7$, so $630 \div 9 = 70$
   d) $60 \div 12 = 5$, so $600 \div 12 = 50$

4. a) Binoculars: $12 \times 6 = 72$, so £$12 \times 60 =$ £720.
      Watches: $3 \times 9 = 27$, so £$300 \times 9 =$ £2700.
   b) $49 \div 7 = 7$, so $490 \div 7 = 70$ disguises

An Extra Challenge

• The only price that can be divided by 500
  is £4500, so this jewel can't be the fake.

• Both 3600 and 5400 can be divided by 900, but
  4200 can't, so the £4200 jewel can't be the fake.

• Out of the two left, only 3600 can be divided
  by 400, so the £3600 jewel can't be the fake.

So the £5400 jewel must be the fake.

Pages 8-9 — More Times Tables Tricks

1. $4 \times 5 \times 2 = 20 \times 2 = 40$
   $4 \times 7 \times 5 = 4 \times 5 \times 7 = 20 \times 7 = 140$
   $4 \times 1 = 4$ $0 \times 5 = 0$
   $2 \times 9 \times 4 = 2 \times 4 \times 9 = 8 \times 9 = 72$
   $6 \times 2 \times 7 = 12 \times 7 = 84$

2. $584 \times 1 = 584$ $719 \times 0 = 0$ $263 \div 1 = 263$

3. a) $2 \times 9 \times 6 = 2 \times 6 \times 9 = 12 \times 9 = 108$
   b) $3 \times 7 \times 4 = 3 \times 4 \times 7 = 12 \times 7 = 84$
   c) $5 \times 8 \times 7 = 40 \times 7 = 280$

4. $5 \times 11 \times 4 = 5 \times 4 \times 11 = 20 \times 11 = 220$
   $6 \times 12 \times 5 = 6 \times 5 \times 12 = 30 \times 12 = 360$

5. a) $3 \times 4 \times 12 = 12 \times 12 = 144$ miles
   b) $3 \times 4 \times 40 = 12 \times 40 = 480$ miles

An Extra Challenge

There are 3 different ways:
$5 \times 8 \times 9 = 40 \times 9 = 360$
$6 \times 6 \times 10 = 36 \times 10 = 360$
$2 \times 20 \times 9 = 40 \times 9 = 360$

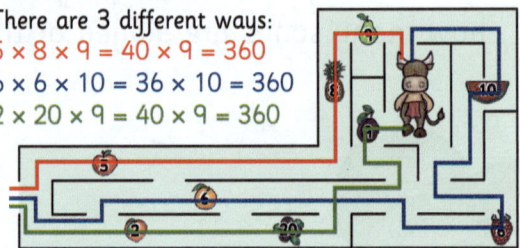

Pages 10-11 — Factor Pairs

1. 12 → 2, 6   15 → 5, 3   21 → 7, 3

2. 33 —— 3 —— 11 $(3 \times 11 = 33)$
   25 —— 5 —— 5 $(5 \times 5 = 25)$
   10 —— 2 —— 5 $(2 \times 5 = 10)$
   36 —— 6 —— 6 $(6 \times 6 = 36)$

3. 5 and **12** are a factor pair of 60. $(5 \times 12 = 60)$
   7 and 8 are a factor pair of **56**. $(7 \times 8 = 56)$

4. a) 1 and 18   2 and 9   3 and 6
   b) There are 4 different ways. (2 groups of 9, or
      9 groups of 2, or 3 groups of 6, or 6 groups of 3).

5. 20 people can be split into: 2 groups of 10, or
   10 groups of 2, or 4 groups of 5, or 5 groups of 4.
   So 2, 4, 5 and 10 should be circled.

An Extra Challenge

For example:

It doesn't matter
which way round
you write the factors,
as along as the
correct pair is
below each number.

Answers

Pages 12-13 — Multiplying Using Partitioning

1. a) $32 \times 6 = 30 \times 6 + 2 \times 6 = 180 + 12 = 192$
   b) $56 \times 7 = 50 \times 7 + 6 \times 7 = 350 + 42 = 392$

2. 8×45 ——— 360 4×64 ——— 256
   5×92 ——— 460 6×49 ——— 294
   ($8 \times 45 = 8 \times 40 + 8 \times 5 = 320 + 40 = 360$
   $4 \times 64 = 4 \times 60 + 4 \times 4 = 240 + 16 = 256$
   $5 \times 92 = 5 \times 90 + 5 \times 2 = 450 + 10 = 460$
   $6 \times 49 = 6 \times 40 + 6 \times 9 = 240 + 54 = 294$)

3. a) $£27 \times 9 = £20 \times 9 + £7 \times 9 = £180 + £63 = £243$
   b) $£32 \times 8 = £30 \times 8 + £2 \times 8 = £240 + £16 = £256$

4. $215 \times 3 = 200 \times 3 + 10 \times 3 + 5 \times 3$
   $= 600 + 30 + 15 = 645$
   $172 \times 4 = 100 \times 4 + 70 \times 4 + 2 \times 4$
   $= 400 + 280 + 8 = 688$

5. $125 \times 5 = 100 \times 5 + 20 \times 5 + 5 \times 5$
   $= 500 + 100 + 25 = 625$ portions

An Extra Challenge

Multiply the prices by 25 and find 3 that add up to 300.
You could have:
$£3 \times 25 + £4 \times 25 + £5 \times 25$
$= £75 + £100 + £125 = £300$

Or you could have:
$£2 \times 25 + £7 \times 25 + £3 \times 25$
$= £50 + £175 + £75 = £300$

Pages 14-15 — Kooky Card Game

In Round 1, Raj scores $21 \times 3 = 63$. In Round 2, Abi scores $11 \times 8 = 88$. For Hanna to win both rounds she must play:
- Spaghettling with ×2 in Round 1, to score $32 \times 2 = 64$.
- Skinny Pete with ×4 in Round 2, to score $23 \times 4 = 92$.

In Round 3, Raj scores $160 \div 4 = 40$.
In Round 4, Abi scores $63 \div 7 = 9$.
For Hanna to win Round 3 and lose Round 4 she must play:
- Butter Bye Bye with ÷2 in Round 3, to get $90 \div 2 = 45$.
- The Pattersons with ÷6 in Round 4, to get $48 \div 6 = 8$.

Pages 16-17 — The Grid Method

1.
×	6
100	600
80	480
	1080

×	5
100	500
90	450
2	10
	960

×	4
200	800
60	240
3	12
	1052

2.
×	3
300	900
40	120
7	21
	1041

×	7
100	700
50	350
2	14
	1064

×	8
100	800
20	160
6	48
	1008

3.
×	6
400	2400
80	480
3	18
	2898

2898 ✓

4. a) $39 \times £8$

×	8
30	240
9	72
	312

So Renee spent £312.

b) $124 \times £9$

×	9
100	900
20	180
4	36
	1116

So Tim spent £1116.

An Extra Challenge

They can see 12 butterflies.
You need to calculate 27×12:

×	12
20	240
7	84
	324

So there are 324 butterflies.

Pages 18-19 — Written Multiplication 1

1.
```
    6 5
  ×   7
    3 5
  4 2 0
  4 5 5
```
```
    8 9
  ×   2
    1 8
  1 6 0
  1 7 8
```
```
    3 6
  ×   9
    5 4
  2 7 0
  3 2 4
      1
```

2.
```
    3 5 7
  ×     4
      2 8
    2 0 0
  1 2 0 0
  1 4 2 8
```
1428

3. A
```
    1 8 9
  ×     6
      5 4
    4 8 0
    6 0 0
  1 1 3 4
      1
```
B
```
    2 6 7
  ×     4
      2 8
    2 4 0
    8 0 0
  1 0 6 8
```
C
```
    3 5 2
  ×     3
        6
    1 5 0
    9 0 0
  1 0 5 6
```

4.
```
    7 4 2
  ×     3
        6
    1 2 0
  2 1 0 0
  2 2 2 6
```
```
    4 9 4
  ×     5
      2 0
    4 5 0
  2 0 0 0
  2 4 7 0
```
```
    5 1 7
  ×     8
      5 6
      8 0
  4 0 0 0
  4 1 3 6
      1
```

Answers

An Extra Challenge

Super Cluckers:
```
    9 3
×     6
    1 8
  5 4 0
  5 5 8
```

Snowies:
```
    2 6 8
×       3
      2 4
    1 8 0
    6 0 0
    8 0 4
      1
```

Fancy Feathers:
```
    1 9 4
×       4
      1 6
    3 6 0
    4 0 0
    7 7 6
```

Red Hens:
```
    1 5 7
×       5
      3 5
    2 5 0
    5 0 0
    7 8 5
```

So the Snowies have laid the largest number of eggs.

Pages 20-21 — Written Multiplication 2

1.
```
    8 3
×     6
  4 9 8
    1
```
```
    1 9 7
×       4
    7 8 8
    3 2
```
```
    4 5 8
×       3
  1 3 7 4
    1 2
```

2.
```
    1 5 7
×       8
  1 2 5 6
    4 5
```
```
    1 3 2
×       9
  1 1 8 8
    2 1
```
```
    2 4 4
×       6
  1 4 6 4
    2 2
```

The shortest route is ✓ Paleo Path.

3.
```
    3 7 6
×       3
  1 1 2 8
    2 1
```
So the fake is ↗

4.
```
    1 6 2
×       9
  1 4 5 8
    5 1
```
So 1458 bones.

5.
```
    3 4 8
×       7
  2 4 3 6
    3 5
```
So £2436.

An Extra Challenge

Try each square until you find the multiplication that gives 324.

It's 🦴 as 36 × 9 = 324.
```
    3 6
×     9
  3 2 4
    5
```

Pages 22-23 — Dividing Using Partitioning

1. 300 ÷ 3 = 100
   18 ÷ 3 = 6
   So 318 ÷ 3 = 106

   800 ÷ 4 = 200
   24 ÷ 4 = 6
   So 824 ÷ 4 = 206

2. a) 96 ÷ 6 = 16   b) 85 ÷ 5 = 17   c) 91 ÷ 7 = 13

3. 118 ÷ 2 ——— 59   428 ÷ 4 ——— 107
   336 ÷ 3 ——— 112   255 ÷ 5 ——— 51
   (118 ÷ 2 = 100 ÷ 2 + 18 ÷ 2 = 50 + 9 = 59
   428 ÷ 4 = 400 ÷ 4 + 28 ÷ 4 = 100 + 7 = 107
   336 ÷ 3 = 300 ÷ 3 + 36 ÷ 3 = 100 + 12 = 112
   255 ÷ 5 = 200 ÷ 5 + 55 ÷ 5 = 40 + 11 = 51)

4. a) 315 ÷ 3 = 300 ÷ 3 + 15 ÷ 3 = 100 + 5 = 105 km
   b) 315 ÷ 5 = 300 ÷ 5 + 15 ÷ 5 = 60 + 3 = 63 km

An Extra Challenge

The useful calculations are: 350 ÷ 7 and 21 ÷ 7
(as 350 + 21 = 371 and 7 divides both 350 and 21).
350 ÷ 7 = 50 and 21 ÷ 7 = 3, so 371 ÷ 3 = 53.

Pages 24-25 — Written Division

1. 72 ÷ 4
```
      1 8
  4 ⟌ 7 ³2
```
98 ÷ 7
```
      1 4
  7 ⟌ 9 ²8
```
84 ÷ 6
```
      1 4
  6 ⟌ 8 ²4
```

2.
```
      1 1 1
  5 ⟌ 5 5 5
```
```
      1 3 5
  7 ⟌ 9 ²4 ³5
```
```
      1 7 1
  4 ⟌ 6 ²8 4
```
```
      1 3 4
  6 ⟌ 8 ²0 ²4
```

3. (560 ÷ 5)   (448 ÷ 4)   (784 ÷ 7)   226 ÷ 2
```
      1 1 2
  5 ⟌ 5 6 ¹0
```
```
      1 1 2
  4 ⟌ 4 4 8
```
```
      1 1 2
  7 ⟌ 7 8 ¹4
```
```
      1 1 3
  2 ⟌ 2 2 6
```

4.
```
      9 4
  4 ⟌ 3 ³7 ³6
```
So there are 94 places in each field.

An Extra Challenge

a)
```
      6 3
  2 ⟌ 1 ¹2 6
```
Yes, 63 groups of 2.

b)
```
      4 2
  3 ⟌ 1 ¹2 6
```
Yes, 42 groups of 3.

c) Find numbers that divide 126. They could split into groups of: **6** (21 groups), **7** (18 groups), or **9** (14 groups). Use factor pairs to find more: **14** (9 groups), **18** (7 groups), **21** (6 groups), **42** (3 groups), or **63** (2 groups).

Pages 26-27 — Real-Life Problems

1. a)
```
      1 4 5
×         8
    1 1 6 0   invitations
      3 4
```
b)
```
        1 7 7   replies
  3 ⟌ 5 ²3 ²1
```

2.
```
      4 9 0
×         8
    3 9 2 0   So £3920.
      7
```

3. There are 62 × 8 = 496 chairs in total.
   So 496 − 490 = 6 chairs are spare.
   The group of 6 chairs should be circled.
```
      6 2
×       8
    4 9 6
      1
```

4. 5 hours = 5 × 60 = 300 minutes
   300 ÷ 3 = 100 songs

An Extra Challenge

24 small bunches is 24 × 3 = 72 balloons.
13 large bunches is 13 × 8 = 104 balloons.
So 346 − 72 − 104 = 170 balloons come from medium bunches.
170 ÷ 5 = 34 medium bunches.
```
    2 4
×     3
    7 2
    1
```
```
    1 3
×     8
  1 0 4
    2
```
```
      3 4
  5 ⟌ 1 ¹7 ²0
```